GETTING YOUR HEALTH MINISTRY UP AND GROWING: A GUIDE FOR FAITH COMMUNITY NURSES

GETTING YOUR HEALTH MINISTRY UP AND GROWING: A GUIDE FOR FAITH COMMUNITY NURSES

Angel Smothers

ISBN-13: 9780692773215
ISBN-10: 0692773215

Table of Contents

Introduction

Sometimes the Lord will put it on your heart in which direction He wants you to go in your life and sometimes He waits on you to step out and start walking before He gives you guidance. Sometimes we are so busy with living life we don't hear His directions. It reminds me of when we are driving somewhere using a GPS. We get so tired of hearing the directions when we know where we are going that we turn the volume down. The next thing we know we have missed a turn because we were still relying on our own directions that had run out. Life can be that way. We think we have a plan and find out abruptly that our plan isn't going to happen after all. I know that I have had this happen on more than one occasion. I have a plan and am working towards MY goals and find myself flat on my face, seeking God's Will and guidance. Each time this happens I make a commitment to stay more in tuned and have ears that hear the small still voice; but the further I get from the fall that made me listen in the first place, the harder it is to hear. The Bible tells us to be glad during times of trial and testing. From my experience, those times do help you to be a better listener for God's voice.

. Some of the more trying examples of times when God has provided me with guidance and I haven't listened include changes that He wanted to happen in my career. Most of my life I have been the type of person who is head strong and motivated. I would find a way to achieve something especially if the odds were against me. I wanted to make things happen in my life that no one could see coming and no one would have expected from me. I grew up in a home with parents who didn't attend church and the only experiences with church we had as kids was Bible school in the summer. So my idea of listening for God's Will was not in tune with the station He uses which we call the Holy Spirit. I depended on myself and for many, many years that got me where I wanted to be. But there comes a time when depending on yourself doesn't cut it any longer and we have to learn to lean on God. Sometimes He uses painful events in our lives as a time to gain our attention. There is no better time for Him to get our attention than during a time when we have fallen in desperation and pain at the foot of the cross. I am telling you these things because most people are so busy living life that they forget to stop and smell the roses AND to see the big picture. We are here on earth for a short time. We are visitors here and on our way home to a better place. We must avoid getting wrapped up in the ins and outs of this world and consider closely every day what we are supposed to be doing for the good of God's kingdom.

Pause for Prayer
Add to the following prayer based on what's on your heart right now. Father thank you for all that you have given me and all that You are using me for in Your kingdom...

_____

_____

_____

_____

1

Listening for That Small Still Voice

SPIRITUAL GIFTS

I Corinthians 12: 4-11

⁴There are different kinds of gifts, but the same Spirit distributes them. ⁵ There are different kinds of service, but the same Lord. ⁶ There are different kinds of working, but in all of them and in everyone it is the same God at work.

⁷ Now to each one the manifestation of the Spirit is given for the common good.⁸ To one there is given through the Spirit a message of wisdom, to another a message of knowledge by means of the same Spirit, ⁹ to another faith by the same Spirit, to another gifts of healing by that one Spirit, ¹⁰ to another miraculous powers, to another prophecy, to another distinguishing between spirits, to another speaking in different kinds of tongues, and to still another the interpretation of tongues. ¹¹ All these are the work of one and the same Spirit, and he distributes them to each one, just as he determines.

Spiritual gifts are things that each of us have been blessed with from God. We are all different and have different gifts that we could use for the work that God wants us to do here. However, our spiritual gifts are also things that can further our own selfish purposes for this world. I know I was guilty of using my spiritual gifts for my own purposes. If you haven't taken a spiritual assessment in the past, I would encourage you to take the time now to do that. Knowing what gifts God has given you can make a huge difference in your life. I found out that my top three spiritual gifts are giving, helps, and encouragement. I didn't know that these were my identified gifts but I knew that I was always a giving person and that I loved to encourage others, but the helps piece is where I found myself living by the flesh. I had an approval addiction and wanted to do as much as I could to show how much my work was worth. I signed up for projects, and committees that were unproductive. I agreed to do work that was above and beyond and stretched myself too thin, all for my own gratification. I guess we could call that pride. I would get into something and then get burned out and not finish it. Because I was an eager person, I had all kinds of people asking for different help; and I thought I was obligated to help because this would keep my fleshly image of self high. I wasn't listening to God and wasn't really even trying. I wanted God to anoint the work that I wanted to do instead of me doing the work that He had anointed me to do. You can see why it took God knocking me down to get me to listen. You hear people talking about having a well moment, but I am here to tell you that I had a Paul moment. I was knocked off a high horse just the same as Paul.

Reflection
Is there a time in your life that you feel God knocked you off of your horse to gain your attention? If so, share how that affected your life both short and long term.

_____

_____

_____

_____

_____

IDENTIFYING GOD'S PLAN

Acts 9: 1-6

Meanwhile, Saul was still breathing out murderous threats against the Lord's disciples. He went to the high priest ² and asked him for letters to the synagogues in Damascus, so that if he found any there who belonged to the Way, whether men or women, he might take them as prisoners to Jerusalem.³ As he neared Damascus on his journey, suddenly a light from heaven flashed around him. ⁴ He fell to the ground and heard a voice say to him, "Saul, Saul, why do you persecute me?"

⁵ "Who are you, Lord?" Saul asked.

"I am Jesus, whom you are persecuting," he replied. ⁶ "Now get up and go into the city, and you will be told what you must do."

Where did I find myself once I hit the ground? At the foot of the cross, of course, listening very intently to God and His plan. His plan included me not taking on more than I could do. His plan included me focusing on Him and sitting quietly in His presence. His plan included me depending on Him and not on the World, and His plan included me using my spiritual gifts for His work. When I first started to recognize His plan, I was afraid; but the more I thought about it, the more I started to realize just how much better His plan was for me. As you could imagine, I found myself in shell shock with questions like HOW, WHY, WHEN all running around my mind. You see it took me getting knocked down on the ground to have the desire to look UP! And up is where everything we need is.

There have been so many doors that have opened in my life that I never saw there until they opened. If God hadn't opened those doors, I would have never knocked on them. It was that opened door that invited me in that gave me the courage to explore what is inside. I will tell you that the plan that God has for us is way better than anything we could come up with as a plan. Yet, we so often get caught in the fleshly desire to control our future. We sometimes say we have faith in God; but when it comes time to turn over everything to Him, we freeze. I know I have frozen in fear many times because my plan was being changed. I couldn't imagine how things would work out; because the only way I could envision things working out for the good, was if they worked out my way. Of course, a few times going through this has helped me see that God's plan is always better than mine. I have discovered and accepted that the plan that God has is the one I need to follow. I guess that old saying about age and wisdom does apply because the longer we have lived the more doors we have had shut in our face the more doors we have seen opened by the hand of God. A few better doors can help us to trust God's plan. But our fleshly instinct is still to try and work things out based on the plans we have made. Which brings me back to the horse. Sometimes getting knocked down is the best way for God to help you see that open door He has provided.

Reflection
Consider when you first remember that you wanted to be a nurse or caregiver. Jot down those memories on the lines below.

_____

_____

_____

_____

_____

I knew that I wanted to be a nurse from the time I was 10-years-old. We had a beloved family member who was almost finished with nursing school killed in a tragic car accident. This was a turning point for our family and a time when I can remember truly seeking God's face. You know pain will make you do that. I wanted to be a nurse because she was never going to be. This was where my fleshly desire kicked in. Coming from a family where my parents didn't graduate high school I found myself standing on ground not treaded in the past. With limited support I moved forward one step in front of the other all the way through high school and college to find myself standing at the bedside of a patient. I had made it as a nurse. I now look back and can see the hand of God with each and every step I took; but while I was in school, I don't remember seeking God's will. I had a will and I wanted God to come with me.

NURSING AS A CALLING

> **Romans 15:1** *We who are strong have an obligation to bear with the failings of the weak, and not to please ourselves.*

It is not unusual for nurses to feel a calling to nursing long before they graduate high school. Some of the spiritual gifts that God, through the Holy Spirit, plants in us; and are there from birth, are stronger in some than others. Some great nurses didn't know they wanted to be a nurse and never felt a calling to nursing until they were well into completing a different degree in college. While others, like myself, knew at a young age that I wanted to be a nurse. Not only that I wanted to be a nurse but that I was supposed to be a nurse. This knowing helped to strengthen and guide me along the way. Remember, I was raised by parents who didn't attend church, so my knowledge of the Holy Spirit's work was minimal. Yet, I still felt a calling for me to grow closer to God. I knew all along that I needed God in my life but without the example of my parents it took me a little longer to return that call from God. Once I realized He had been calling me all of my life, I felt close and connected to Him. It was that first realization that saved me. I not only returned the call to God, but I started to seek Him and His Will.

Seeking God's will can be an encouraging and strengthening part of our lives. We know we need God and we know we want His will but it can be very discouraging if we don't feel we are able to identify what His will is. It is a common struggle for many to hear and understand God's will in their lives. People doubt that they have heard from God. They freeze with fear that they are hearing their own will and not God's; yet, the Bible encourages us to step out in faith and God will direct our paths. This is a common struggle for many, but I often hear nurses say they feel lost regarding what they should be doing with their talents. Many nurses are unsatisfied with their current positions. Many nurses change positions often due to this feeling, and even more often nurses remain in positions with which they are not happy. Many unhappy nurses are also non-Christian nurses, but a large number of unhappy nurses are Christians who attend church on a regular bases. When asked why they are unhappy with their current nursing position they often cite things such as work hours, or limited flexibility. Often nurses will tell you they don't feel they are doing the type of nursing that God has called them to do. With the aging population of baby boomers, we are approaching a health care crisis with more elderly people needing care then there are nurses available to provide that care. Unhappy nurses, many of which are leaving nursing all together, don't help to strengthen the healthcare team for this upcoming care crisis.

Reflection
Have you ever felt that God was calling you in a different direction from the one that you were currently moving towards? If so how did you handle this change?

_____

_____

_____

_____

_____

_____

It is during these times of calling that we as nurses can often lose sight of what our personal goals as a member of the body of Christ are. We have to listen for that small still voice and step out in faith, with total faith that the Lord WILL direct our path.

Proverbs 16:3
Commit to the LORD whatever you do, and he will establish your plans.

Let's pretend for a minute that we all have heard that small still voice, we have interpreted what it means for our lives, we have stepped out in faith working toward God's will in our lives, and we have reached the level where we are able to see the fruits of our labor in God's will. What a wonderful place that would be for us all. However, the truth is; the major-ity of us are still working toward this goal. We are at different levels of this process and we all get entangled and held up at different levels of this process. Some of us will hear God's will and immediately feel comfortable that we have heard from God; while others of us, me included, will doubt over and over that we have heard from Him. However, that same person who knew they had heard from God and moved forward may get trapped and held back before they ever see the fruits of their labor. I think that the more we share in our struggles the more we will be able to support and encourage each other towards meeting exceptional levels of accomplishment for the Kingdom of God.

Pause for Prayer

Finish the following prayer with words that are on your heart right now. Father you have been a blessing to me and through me; now I.....

_____

_____

_____

_____

WHY START A HEALTH MINISTRY?

It is for this reason that I have felt guided by God to write these ideas down to share with my brothers and sisters in Christ. Because I have struggled with recognizing my role in the Kingdom, it might help if I share my ideas and stories with you with the prayer and hope that you will work through this book and in turn use it to help other nurses who are struggling as well. When we start to recognize that we are a team as fellow brothers and sisters in Christ, we are stronger for each other. Now let's consider this upcoming crisis in healthcare. We know that the aging population and the overall nursing shortage will meet in the middle within the next 10 years. We will see more and more chronically ill elderly and aging members of our congregation and our communities but less and less nursing support available. As we are faced with these issues, it will be necessary for nurses within the Body of Christ to step up and help to meet the needs of these aging children of God. As with any crisis, things work out best if we identify the upcoming potential issue and work early to address it. As nurses and members of the Body of Christ, we have a calling to support and encourage one another as well as those in the communities who are also God's children. There is a model of care that has been in place for many years which is known by different names: Parish nursing, health ministry, faith community nursing, or wellness ministry. Either of these terms can be used to define the role of the nurse working amongst the congregation with the goal of promoting health and comfort.

Reflection

How would you envision your role as a nurse working amongst a congregation? What are some things that you feel would be helpful for you to do?

_____

_____

_____

_____

_____

_____

_____

WHAT IS A FAITH COMMUNITY NURSE?

A Faith Community Nurse(FCN) is a nurse who works within a faith community. In the past you might have heard this role termed parish nurse. This is a still a term you may hear in today's times as well. A faith community nurse is a nurse who works within a faith community providing education and support of health-related needs. FCN's do not do hands-on care. This means you would not expect an FCN to administer injections, or do wound care. However, you might expect them to educate on how to self-administer insulin or do a non-sterile dressing change at home.

The role of the FCN has been well defined over the past thirty plus years. The ANA has developed a guide for the FCN which details their expected roles within a congregation. There are many FCNs working within their places of worship who have no additional training related to their role as an FCN. However, the current standard would be for each nurse to complete an FCN training program through the Church Health Center. The CHC is a wonderful resource for the FCN. They oversee and guide the FCN curriculum that is used to educate nurses in the role of the FCN. There are programs all across the country that educate FCNs using this curriculum. The content is the same within these programs but the delivery methods can vary. For example, there are some programs that require a one-week commitment each day for a week. There are other programs that require two weekends to complete the requirements. There are also self-paced online programs as well as hybrid programs where some of the content is online and some in person. Each of these programs have benefits and each nurse should consider their needs before applying to a program. Also, there is no rule against taking two of the programs. I completed an online version of the program and then in a year did an onsite version. I learned new information from both methods.

GETTING STARTED

Isaiah 30:21

Whether you turn to the right or to the left, your ears will hear a voice behind you, saying, "This is the way; walk in it."

When considering a health ministry, several beginning steps should be completed to strengthen the foundation of the program. To start with, a passion from one or more nurses to develop a health ministry is imperative. There are often nurses within a congregation who have different strengths that supplement a health ministry. We will talk about those later. Identifying all of the nurses in a congregation who have a passion to serve as members of the health ministry team will allow ideas to flow early in the development process. Once those nurses are identified, then a health ministry planning committee should be formed. On the planning committee should be those nurses who are interested; as well as, the church secretary; other health care team members; and lay person members of the congregation. A planning committee of 5-10 people will keep it small enough for close contact. Once those congregation members have been identified, an email or other preferred contact should be sent letting them know that their agreement to participate on the health ministry planning committee is not a commitment to serve as an active member of the health ministry. Sometimes people are overextended and are not comfortable volunteering, so letting them know this is an agreement to serve on a planning committee with limited meetings may help strengthen the planning committee.

Reflection
Consider your congregation and who you might consider asking to serve as a member of the planning committee and make notes below.

_____
_____
_____
_____

Once you have developed the planning committee, setting up the first meeting will be next. This meeting should be in a central location that has access for all members. The church conference room or office would work. Provide them with multiple options and consider using the online tool for scheduling meetings called "Doodle Link". This is a free source to allow you to develop an easy email based meeting availability schedule. Once the meeting is set you would want to develop an agenda for the meeting. See below a possible agenda for the meeting.

Discussion Agenda:

- Discussion regarding feasibility of forming a health ministry at our church
- Discussion regarding the role of a faith community nurse and a health ministry
- Discussion regarding how such a ministry should unfold
- Discussion regarding phases of development

Notes:

_____
_____
_____
_____
_____
_____

Once the agenda is developed, send it out to the planning committee and ask that they consider their thoughts on these agenda items before the first meeting.

2

Moving Forward

PLANNING COMMITTEE MEETING

Open the first planning committee meeting with prayer asking the Lord to guide you in sharing your thoughts on the development of a health ministry at your church. Move forward with an introduction from each committee member and their position on the committee. These positions might include: nurse, other health care member, lay person etc. During the meeting spend time getting to know the ideas and visions of the members of the planning committee. This is a good time for the members to make note of concerns, fears and perceived obstacles regarding development of a health ministry. During this meeting careful notes should be taken. Within a few days after the meeting the notes from the meeting should be sent to each of the committee members for review before moving forward with sharing the committees work with the Pastor and later the church board. See below potential notes from the first planning committee meeting.

Summary of Discussion Points from Planning Committee Meeting 1:

- All agree that a health ministry would be a nice addition to the other ministries at our church
- Each committee member agrees that we should start small and move slow with the ministry development and growth
- Each member felt that moving and expanding in phases would work best for growth
- Member A made note of the importance of staying focused in the group and having clear expectations for how and what we will do
- Member B made note of the important role of the non-healthcare trained people in this ministry
- Member C made note of the importance of having a plan to collect information and suggestions from the congregation in a structured format
- Member D made note of the importance of having a plan for how to address situations when we encounter them

- Member E felt that home visits were an important part of the ministry and should be included in phase one
- Member B also made note of the importance of identifying ways we are already doing similar activities and incorporate those activities and volunteers in the health ministry

Reflection
__Consider the types of questions that you would like to ask as a member of a future health ministry planning committee and include them below__

_____

_____

_____

_____

_____

_____

As a part of the first planning committee meeting a phase 1 proposal should be developed which details how the planning committee envisions the health ministry to unfold. Starting with a phase 1 that is the first 6 months of the ministry will allow the pastor and church board members to envision how the ministry would unfold. This is an important first step and should be a doable plan that doesn't start with lofty ideas. Start slow and move slow. Overwhelming yourself or other volunteers to early could result in failure of the ministry.

Psalm 61:2 From the end of the earth I will cry to You, When my heart is overwhelmed; Lead me to the rock that is higher than I.

Proposed Phase 1: Timeframe Six months

- Approval of the ministry with the church board: Scheduled for next board meeting

- Planning Committee second meeting with development of a budget
- Introduction of the ministry to the congregation with a planned survey through an online survey tool
- Blood pressure screening policy development
- Blood Pressure screenings on select Sundays after service
- Schedule health education sessions based on needs assessment survey
- Pilot home visits with those in the congregation who are in need

Reflection

Consider the above phase 1 plan. List items that you feel could be realistic for a health ministry at your church and also parts of the phase 1 plan that you don't feel you could accomplish in the first 6 months of the ministry.

_____

_____

_____

_____

_____

_____

_____

TAKING YOUR PLAN TO THE PASTOR AND CHURCH BOARD

After the planning committee meeting you would want to make an appointment with your pastor to discuss the committees report. During this meeting providing the Pastor with details of what a health ministry is and how it would unfold will allow them to envision the role of such a ministry amongst the congregation. If the Pastor agrees with the planning committees plans your next step would be to take the report before the Church Board allowing a decision to be made in regards to the feasibility of a health ministry. If the church board approves the health ministry as a new ministry at your church you will continue on with the steps in the phase I plan.

Reflection

What are some questions that you would anticipate the church board asking you regarding a health ministry?

_____

_____

_____

_____

_____

_____

_____

BUDGETING

The first step of phase one would be the development of a budget for the upcoming first year of the health ministry. Start with having the planning committee offering suggestions of those supplies and funds that would be needed during the first year. Then develop a budget and send out to the planning committee for approval before forwarding it to the appropriate finance person. See potential year 1 budget below.

Health Ministry Budget Proposal: Year 1

- 2 Blood Pressure Cuffs (that we keep in a box and use the same ones each time we check a BP) $50
- Glucometer and test strips (for later in the year) $50
- Copies $20
- Paper $10
- BP Tracking Cards $20
- Hand sanitizer $20
- Box of Gloves $20
- Sharps Box $20
- Business cards with our name and email $50
- Unknown Needs $150

Total Requested $410 for the year

Reflection

Consider items that you would need for your first year in the health ministry and make a list below.

_____

_____

_____

_____

_____

_____

Some common items that other faith community nurses have made note of using in their health ministry programs are as follows:

1- Blood pressure cuff and stethoscope
2- Locked filing cabinet area
3- Other storage for educational materials
4- Office Supplies
5- Access to copier and fax machine

FUNDRAISING:

When developing the budget for a new health ministry program you would also want to consider how the health ministry team might contribute toward the budget needs. Consider fundraising ideas as a group with the planning committee. Some possible ideas are listed below:

1- Bake Sale
2- Car Wash
3- Selling items for a fund raising company
4- Hosting a dinner at the church

Consider a list of fundraising ideas you have worked with in the past and make a list below. Then add ideas you might have for new ways to raise funds to support a new health ministry.

_____

_____

_____

_____

_____

_____

FORMING THE TEAM

Proverbs 27:17 _Iron sharpens iron, and one man sharpens another._

Once you have received approval from the church board and have a budget in place it is time to recruit team members to serve on the health ministry team. Not to get confused with the health ministry planning committee. The planning committee has done its job. That's not to say that some of the members from the planning committee might not be on the health ministry team.

The health ministry team will consist of volunteers that work as a part of the team for the purpose of meeting the goals outlined in the previous sections. The team should consist of a variety of church members including nursing, medicine, therapy, and lay person. The team members will each bring strength to the team based on their personal experiences and spiritual gifts.

When considering the work that the health ministry team will do it is important to consider how to best recruit, educate and retain volunteers. Because it is best to have health ministry volunteers functioning within their spiritual gifting it would be important to plan a training session that includes a spiritual gifting test. In addition to the spiritual gifting test you would also want to educate them on the importance of confidentiality. See below for a sample detailed agenda for an education session for potential volunteers.

VOLUNTEER TRAINING

1- Introduction that include each person's personal interest and passion. Also include why each person has an interest in volunteering for the health ministry team.

2- Discuss the role of a health ministry within a congregation and make note of the findings from the work of the health ministry planning committee.
3- Each person should complete a spiritual gifting assessment and discussion regarding the results.
4- Ask each member how they would envision their work as a member of the health ministry team.
5- Educate on the importance of confidentiality and have each volunteer sign that they received this education.
6- Plan a second education session where new questions and concerns can be addressed and those who remain interested in being a volunteer can attend.

Reflection
Spend time making a list of other potential discussion points that you would like to make with the volunteers at the training session

_____
_____
_____
_____
_____
_____

Each health ministry team will function differently based on a variety of factors. A health ministry team who is coordinated by a non-paid volunteer nurse will function differently than a team that is coordinated by a paid nurse. We will discuss this further later in the book. Also considering how many volunteers come forward will determine the feasibility of how involved the health ministry may become. Timing is important. Early in the development and unfolding of a health ministry there may be obstacles that were not foreseen that must be overcome. These obstacles could potentially halt progression of the ministries work all together. Below is a list of potential activities a health ministry team may plan for, but again the number of volunteers and the amount of time the health ministry nurse coordinator can devote to the ministry will dictate this.

1- Blood pressure screenings after morning service
2- Quarterly newsletter that covers main ideas for the health and wellness of the congregation
3- Monthly or quarterly education sessions that are based on congregation suggestion. These can be held on a Tuesday evening at the church and should be open to both the congregation and the community
4- Develop a bulletin board that rotates education on different topics
5- Have a nurse available to meet one on one with individuals or families from the congregation to discuss health related needs

6- Health ministry home visitation program for the nurse
7- Health ministry home visitations program for the lay person health ministry team volunteer
8- Annual health fair (will discuss in more detail later)

Reflection

Consider which of the above you would like to develop in your congregation and make note of ideas you have for making this happen. Also list any ideas that you have that are not on the list

_____

_____

_____

_____

_____

The above is a list of possible ideas. This doesn't mean that each health ministry team would start out doing them all. In fact the majority of long term successful health ministry programs start low and go slow. This means they are realistic about what they will actually be able to accomplish. It might be that they start with just a blood pressure session monthly and expand from there. It is also important that your planning be fluid. This means that you would want to be flexible as a team making sure to have opportunities for change when needed. This makes it important to know the needs and wants of the congregation. For example you wouldn't want to devote a month of education on the topic of breast feeding if 95% of the congregation are over the age of 60. Instead a topic on stroke prevention and early detection would be a better fit. You would want to start this process with a survey of the congregation. You would want to collect data that you could use to tailor your education and outreach plans for the year. See the sample congregation survey link in the resource section at the end of the book.

Reflection

Now spend time considering items from the sample survey that you would like to know and plan for early in the health ministry development at your church. It might be that you have multiple surveys over the first year and that you start with a smaller simpler one. Also list any data you might want to collect that was not included above.

_____

_____

_____

_____

_____

Before you administer the survey it is important to consider the best options for collecting these data. For example within a smaller congregation with mainly elderly members the use of online technology to administer the survey may lead to a low response rate. However if you are working with a congregation of primarily young adult families the use of online polling might help to obtain the best poll response rate. Tools such as a survey monkey could be used to collect the online data. This is a free service and the survey could be sent out by email.

Reflection

Consider the best method to polling your congregation and make note of your ideas below.

_____

_____

_____

_____

3

Getting the Word Out

ANNOUNCING THE HEALTH MINISTRY TO THE CONGREGATION

As with most new programs the word will spread through the congregation rather early that a new ministry is in the works. This is a normal response to new ideas and changes. When the health ministry planning committee first meet as a group, a small amount of questions will surface and can lead to many questions as the startup of the health ministry approaches. Take this word of mouth and use it to your advantage. Be prepared to answer questions and share ideas with those who approach you. Also have a method already planned for allowing members of the church to voice their needs for health related activities. Some ideas for fielding questions and taking suggestions are listed below.

1- Have business cards made with the preferred contact information for each member of the team or just the health ministry team coordinator. Have these cards ready on hand to give out when questions or suggestions come forward. You could use the email method where you request each question or idea be emailed to you. This would only include board suggestions or questions. All individual and private questions should be handled in a personal one on one meeting

2- Have a suggestion box in the foyer of the church

3- Host an open house question and answer session for those interested

Reflection

Consider how you might best approach this within the congregation that you would serve. Make note below and also jot down any additional ideas you might have so far.

_____

_____

_____

_____

_____

GETTING THE WORD OUT

All churches handle announcements differently. Depending on how your church handles announcements you will need to develop a plan for announcing and re-announcing the new health ministry services. Some possible ways to make this announcement are listed below.

1- Church bulletin for 4-6 weeks from the start date of the ministry
2- Weekly church email also 4-6 weeks in advance
3- Newsletters
4- Hanging a flyer on an easily accessible bulletin board
5- Developing flyers to go in mailboxes of the church members
6- Hosting an open house with refreshment

Reflection

The above are all ideas for making the big announcement. Consider which of these would work for your new health ministry program. Make note of these and how you would plan to utilize them. Include any ideas you may have that are not on the list above.

_____
_____
_____
_____
_____

Now that you have officially worked to get the new health ministry program at your church up and running it is time to move into phase 2 of the planning. I can already hear you thinking……..and the answer is NO! Planning is never done. Phase 2 of planning is occurring simultaneously while the health ministry program is getting started. Waiting to plan for phase 2 until long after the health ministry has got started will delay your progress and growth as a ministry of Gods work. Getting started early with this planning will result in strength and stability of the ministry as well as growth. What a shame it would be to get the health ministry off the ground at your church just to watch it slide into nonexistence. I think we have all seen similar things happen with ministries at our church. Early planning may keep this from happening.

I think we are all guilty of taking on more than we can handle or biting off more than we can chew. Developing a health ministry program is no different. Yes God will guide you and support you. Yes God will encourage you and strengthen you. This I know for sure. But He also expects you let some other things go. If you have one plate and it is full it would be really unwise to heap a health ministry on top of the full plate. Instead carefully and prayerfully consider what you could eliminate from your plate to make room for the work that God has called you to do. Nursing is a profession where it can be really difficult to say No! However it is imperative that we get better at this.

Pause For Prayer

Finish the following prayer with words that are on your heart right now. God I want to be available to do your work and not busy doing my own work..........

_____

_____

_____

_____

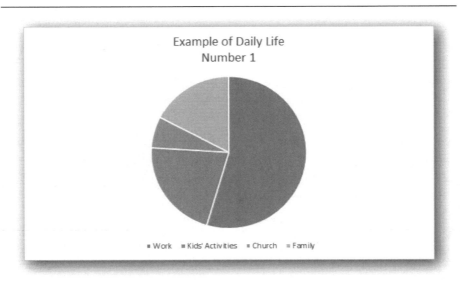

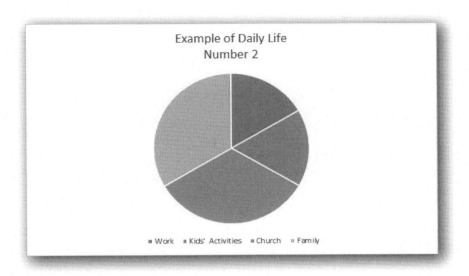

Reflection

Now that you have seen both examples above, carefully consider which plate looks more like yours. Then think of ways that you plan to make room in your life for the work that God has asked you to do. List them below.

_____

_____

_____

_____

_____

Carefully and prayerfully developing a plan to make room in your life for God's work will help to prevent burnout and other complications from taking on too much. Trust me, I am the past queen of taking on too much. It wasn't until God knocked me down that I realized I only need to focus on His Will not my own. But that's another book......

Matthew 7:20 Therefore by their fruits you will know them.

SCHEDULE REGULAR MEETINGS WITH THE TEAM

I don't know about you, but I used to spend the majority of my professional time in meetings. It seems that we had a lot of meetings about the same thing over and over because what we met about never got done. This section will discuss how to develop and keep meetings with the health ministry team that will be productive and fruitful! After all, meetings help us all get on the same page; and, hopefully, will also allow us to encourage each other as a team to keep our plate less full.

When planning meetings, you should keep the meetings less than an hour long. Nothing will run volunteers off faster than long reoccurring and frequent meetings. Start by using a method to check availability of the team members. As mentioned earlier if the team is techno-savvy consider using a tool such as doodle to check group availability for meetings. There is also the old-fashioned and highly-effective use of a phone. Yes, a phone call is still a nice way to set up a meeting. Meetings should be held quarterly unless an emergent need arises. Quarterly meetings allow you and the other members of the team to collect agenda items to discuss at the meeting. Also setting up a group chat via text or google chat can help you to remain accessible to each other. Email can work quite well to keep a group in close contact, also.

Below are examples of quarterly agenda items for Year 1 of a health ministry. Of course, this is just a sample and can and will vary; but it gives you ideas for how your meetings might look.

Meeting 1 Quarter 1
Agenda Items

I.   Discuss how screening and education sessions have been going in the first quarter
II. Review the congregational survey to determine future educational needs
III. Discuss the current list of volunteers and each role
IV. Plan dates for next blood pressure screenings and educational sessions

V.   Develop a summary to provide to the pastor of the number screened and educated (Never include names as this is confidential)

Meeting 2 Quarter 2

I.   Discuss how screening and education sessions have been going in the second quarter
II. Start review of the current year's budget and start planning for the budget for Year 2
III. Discuss current fund-raising efforts
IV. Plan dates for next blood pressure and educational sessions
V.   Develop a summary to provide to the pastor

Meeting 3 Quarter 3

I.   Discuss how screening and educational sessions have been going in the third quarter
II. Start work on planning a yearly health-fair event for congregation and community
III. Take a look at the team's goals for Year 1 and work to develop a list of goals for Year 2. Share these goals with the pastor and church board
IV. Develop a plan for expanding volunteer services
V.   Develop a summary to provide to the pastor

Meeting 4 Quarter 4

I.   Discuss how screening and educational sessions have been going in the third quarter
II. Firm up next year's budget and submit it to the board
III. Health fair to occur in this quarter
IV. Firm up Year 2 goals and start planning for them
V.   Do a health-ministry team retreat to relax and strengthen as a team
VI. Develop a summary to provide to the pastor

Reflection

The sample agenda items for team meetings above can help to get you thinking about how you would host a meeting. On the lines below consider items that you would like to see on the agenda for each quarter and right them down.

_____

_____

_____

_____

_____

_____

KEEPING THE PASTOR IN THE LOOP

During the early planning phase of the health ministry, the pastor was involved as you met with the church board and started the planning committee. He/she was also involved as the ministry unfolded. Now that you are moving along with the ministry, you still need to keep the pastor involved in planning or implementing ideas that the health ministry team develop. This is important as the pastor should give approval for all activities related to all ministries within the church. Also he/she serves as a great springboard for ideas. Many times the pastor will guide you in a direction that will result in improved congregational turnout or support for an idea.

4

Steadying the Ship

SCREENING AND EDUCATIONAL PROGRAMS

Often times a health ministry team will coordinate screening events for the congregation. This could include blood pressure screenings before or after worship service or on an alternate day. Screening sessions can also be done as a private one-on-one meeting. No matter how you plan these events you will find that the congregation will be interested in these types of services. You will actually find that a core group of tried and true faithful will emerge who ALWAYS come for screenings. This is great because they often bring a new friend to future screenings. Once you identify those who are consistently coming to health ministry events, consider them your team champions. They are excellent resources for getting the word out. When planning screening events you will want to keep in mind the needs and wants of the congregation. If you have a congregation who primarily consists of young families with children you might find that a bone density screening may not have as successful of a turnout compared to lead in children. Asking the congregation what they want and need is such an important part of a successful health ministry that polling them as often as 3 times a year during the first few years would be recommended. Below is a list of potential screening ideas for your review.

1- Blood pressure screening on a monthly basis before or after church service
2- Vision or hearing screening
3- Dental Screening
4- Bone density screening
5- Breast screening and education
6- Nutritional assessment
7- Screening by the American Diabetic Association
8- Depression Screening

Planning a screening event that corresponds with other nationally recognized health- related events can work out in your favor. For example, a great time to do breast cancer screening and education would be in the month of October. October is national breast and cervical cancer screening month. Depression screening around the holidays is also a good placement. Plan for events months or a year in advance so that you can match up your screening with national events.

When considering the time that could go into planning screening events, it would be easy for a health ministry team member to get overwhelmed and avoid it all together. But there are several tips that I will share with you below that you will find helpful in making the planning of screening events very much doable.

Nursing schools are located all throughout every state in this country. There are traditional BSN programs, Associate degree programs, and LPN programs. Each school of nursing has a set requirement for volunteer hours that students must complete. Having student volunteers on your team can make the difference when it comes to special projects such as screening events. Students can take an idea for a screening event that you have and start the ball rolling. They can contact potential guest speakers. They can also contact national and local associations to set up a screening event. They can help develop educational material and also start the process of announcing the event. All of this work will count toward required volunteer hours for them. This work is also a wonderful way for you to make progress with your health ministry work while serving as a role model for a new nurse.

In addition to nursing students, there are other health-related disciplines that also make great additions to the health ministry volunteer team. Physical therapy students are one example, as well as, dental students. Whatever your screening project, start early and consider the many wonderful options for support you have available in your surrounding community or even right within your congregation. You could use networking within the congregation to ask for support from someone within your church that has a special knowledge or skill that you could use to plan and implement an educational or screening session.

Reflection

Consider your options for support from the congregation or surrounding community for planning and implementing educational and screening events. Make a list below of ideas you have for reaching out to these sources for support for your health ministry activities.

_____

_____

_____

_____

_____

SUPPORT GROUPS

When considering the needs within a congregation, it is also important to consider how the use of a support group setting could benefit members of the church. Support groups can form around any group of people who are facing a challenging situation in common. Some of the more frequently formed support groups include depression and anxiety, grief and bereavement and diabetes and other chronic illnesses. These support groups can serve an educational role related to the community. The support aspect comes in to play when the members are able to provide each other will encouragement. A support group works best if the members are not required to be church members. Often there will be 1-2 people within a congregation that would participate in the support group but there are also many more people who would benefit that do not attend the church. This makes it very important to open participation for support groups to the surrounding communities. For the members of the church to get the full benefit of a support group, there would need to be more than 3 group members. Below is a list of potential support groups.

1- Diabetes support group
2- HIV/AIDS support group
3- Addiction support group

4- Bereavement support group

5- Depression/Anxiety Support group

6- Dementia support group

Support group members are not always those suffering with the actual illness. Families and friends can gain a good deal of support from attending a support group. When someone you love is suffering or struggling with an issue, meeting others who are also struggling and their families can be very comforting. When developing a support group plan, keep this in mind. Assess the needs of families and friends within the congregation.

Reflection

Consider your congregational needs. Develop a list of potential support group needs below. Make note of how you might approach the congregation to determine support group needs.

_____

_____

_____

_____

_____

Phase 3:

SUCCESS IN EARLY MINISTRY

Colossians 1:17 *and he is before all things, and in him all things hold together.*

During the first couple of years of a new health ministry, it is to be expected for the growth rate to range from congregation to congregation. There are times when a new health ministry program will take off right out of the door and become large and sustainable within the first year. This is however not the common example. Most health ministry programs start slow and go slow. This means that for the first year the amount of communication and success of the program may be slow. There may be a limited amount of participation from the congregation. This is the time when encouragement is so very important. Remember that the Lord has called you to this work and He will see you through. Consider how long the Israelites were in the dessert before God allowed them to enter the promise land. God has made promises to us; but often, we will find ourselves waiting on His timing.

Psalms 27:14 Wait for the LORD; be strong, and let your heart take courage; wait for the LORD!

Now let's consider the possible barriers to growth within the first couple of years of a new health ministry.

1- Lack of support from the congregation
2- Lack of support from the church board or pastor
3- Financial barriers
4- Limited volunteer support
5- Knowledge deficit on behalf of the nurse or other team members

These are the most common early barriers. Of these, the one that proves to be common in most new health ministries is the limited volunteer support. A good nurse a health ministry does not make. Yes, a great nurse can lead a new health ministry. Yes, a great nurse can organize and educate. Yes, a great nurse can encourage and support. However, no one can do all of these things in isolation for more than a short time. Building the volunteer team is a foundational need. It should be accomplished early. Other activities and moving forward with the health ministry should be delayed until the team is well built.

Reflection

Consider how you would build a strong health ministry volunteer team. Share your ideas on the line below and include any anticipated obstacles within the congregation that you will serve.

_____

_____

_____

_____

5

Sustainability

REASSESSMENT AND EVALUATION STAGE

Psalms 118: 6 *The LORD is with me; I will not be afraid. What can mere mortals do to me?*

As you move into the second year of your health ministry, you will find this to be a great time for reassessment. Remember that you spent time during the early phase of the health ministry development assessing the congregational needs. Now it is time to reassess. Things change within a congregation. Also as you have educated over the past year, you may find that the educational needs of the congregation have changed. Evaluation of your work is one of the most important aspects of your role as a health ministry nurse. These evaluation data will help other nurses who are planning activities within the health ministry. These same data can help nurses who are planning to start a new health ministry. For example, if you are developing an educational session on Diabetes, it would be important to collect evaluation data before and after the session to assess learning. What I am about to say may be scary to some, so hold tight and hear me out. When you are collecting data related to an activity such as this, it is important to have your project reviewed by a local IRB (Internal Review Board). An IRB is a group of people who will review your plan to make sure that it is safe. This means that no one will be harmed physically or psychological with the evaluation of the project. This is a very important step. First, because it will protect you and the participants; and also because it is required to get your evaluation data published. Remember how I said it was important for you to collect evaluation data and share it with others. The best way to share these data would be publication in a journal. Most journals will require that your plan have been reviewed and approved through an IRB before they will publish it. Plan ahead and contact a local hospital near you to set up a time to talk to the IRB to learn to submit your work for review.

Reflection

Now that you have considered why it is important to have your work and evaluation plan reviewed by an IRB that is local to you, spend time jotting down some of the concerns and fears you have related to this process. I promise you are not alone and everyone reading this right now is also afraid. Make the list and share it with the IRB staff and they will be happy to answer your questions.

_____

_____

_____

_____

_____

SUSTAINING

Joshua 1:9 Have I not commanded you? Be strong and coura-geous. Do not be afraid; do not be discouraged, for the LORD your God will be with you wherever you go.

Once the health ministry is up and running, it is important to consider potential ways to make the health ministry sustainable. When I say sustainable, I am referring to the ability to keep the activities of the health ministry going. Many times a new ministry gets off the ground just to die out within a year. We have all seen this happen. Unfortunately, many of the obstacles mentioned earlier in the book can continue to be issues and lead to the decline of a new ministry. Health ministry requires a good bit of volunteer time and support. Therefore, when considering ways to make the health ministry sustainable, one of the focuses would be on the volunteer pool. As the health ministry grows, so will be the need for growth of the health ministry volunteer team.

This makes it very important to have an ongoing volunteer recruitment initiative. New church members will have come in during the year and many of them are looking for ways to get more involved. This is a wonderful way to incorporate them and also continue to strengthen the health ministry. Not only approaching the new church members but also discussing with others already in the church the many opportunities for volunteer service with the growing health ministry team. Another potential pool of volunteer support would be the youth at the church. Teen groups often have ways to give back through volunteer activities. You could approach the youth leader and discuss ways to get the teens involved in helping with activities with the health ministry. In addition, there are always others in communities who need volunteer hours for different obligations. Consider nursing schools and even local high schools as potential sources of volunteers. I like to develop a monthly theme for the bulletin board at the church that has been designated for the health ministry. These displays can be developed by different college students. For example, when planning to address oral health within the congregation, I have students from the dental school design a display board and come in and put it up. They get required volunteer hours for their training program requirement; and the health ministry gets support from students who have a level of expertise in a certain area. Also, I have found that having them come to our church for volunteer works has led to many of them coming back for a church service. Now talk about a win win. Also God must be thrilled to have some young adults coming and volunteering to support His church.

With all of this said, the importance of sustainability cannot be stressed enough. You must have a plan in place that allows you to keep the ministry moving forward. Think about how God sent Joshua, Caleb, and the others into Canaan. They were there to scout things out and develop a plan. We have to be brave. We are after all doing God's work. We shouldn't lose focus on the fact that the work we do is for God! Sustainability will require fearlessness and persistence. Think about Joshua and keep going with your health ministry.

Reflection

Consider ways that you plan to make your health ministry sustainable. Make a list and even order them based on the ones you think are the most important

_____

_____

_____

_____

_____

_____

PAID VS VOLUNTEER POSITION

As you have or will learn in your faith community nursing training program, there are both volunteer and paid positions for faith community nurses. Both of these options have benefits and obstacles. When considering volunteer positions, the benefits would include those churches working with a limited budget. In other words, all churches. It is actually more likely to start with a volunteer position for the health ministry nurse and after a couple of years of proven success and growth develop a plan to convert the position to a paid one. No matter paid or volunteer all new health ministry programs need to have structure that is consistent with the church health centers recommendations. This is going to make the conversion in the future to a paid position much easier. It is important to start organizing and have a plan for moving forward. There are times when a health ministry program gets started without the background and planning and therefore develops weakly and is forced to grow strong in order to survive long term. Instead, the idea is to start strong with a strong group oriented foundation and then grow stronger from there. What I am saying is to treat both the paid and volunteer position the same as far as the standards and how things are done.

Because of limited budgets it can be difficult to have a paid position but not impossible. In fact, health ministry is growing stronger as we face the challenge of dealing with an aging baby boomer population. There are several potential sources of financial support. Below is a list of potential sources to consider as you look for financial support to pay a salary for a health ministry nurse.

1- Local hospital based support
2- Hospice Agency based support
3- Private donor support
4- Fund raisers

Reflection

Consider potential financial support options that you have and make a list of ideas for funding to support for a paid nurse position on the lines below.

_____

_____

_____

_____

_____

COMMUNITY OUTREACH

Community outreach can be a very meaningful and fulfilling part of the health ministry's work. When members of the church work with the health ministry team to reach others outside of their church, they are acting as Jesus called them to. They are being the hands and feet of our risen savior. Community outreach can take many shapes. Community outreach could include the health fair mentioned earlier. A health ministry team can work together to develop a health fair which provides education and support for the congregation. Also other churches and community members can be invited. The community interaction and outreach can help to demonstrate the Fruits of the Spirit and the Love of God to those who may not see it otherwise. Also, community outreach could include the development of a support group within the church where members of the community are welcome to participate as a part of the group. Health ministry based community outreach can also include working as a team to support the local homeless shelter or soup kitchen. You can be creative in the community outreaches you serve... These can be based on need in your area and also accessibility of volunteers to support the work.

Below is a list of potential community outreach programs to consider for your health ministry.

1- Diaper drive for homeless babies and families
2- Support of the local free or reduced cost clinic with volunteer services

3- Community based screenings including blood pressure
4- Health fair annually
5- Support groups for depression or other chronic illness
6- Grief support groups

Reflection

Consider some potential community outreach activities that might work with your health ministry. Make a list below and jot down ideas you have for getting these activities started.

_____

_____

_____

_____

_____

_____

CONCLUSION

It is every day that we nurses have new ideas and plans to make our patient care better. We strive to improve patient outcomes and experiences. We go the extra mile for our patients and our colleagues. It is within health care settings that we do these things. I am asking you to reconsider where healthcare occurs. Yes, we know that care is provided in hospitals, nursing homes, clinics, patient's homes, just to name a few. But consider a different location. Consider the faith community setting as a place of care. It is my prayer that you are able to take the information from this book and develop a plan for how you can use your God given spiritual gifts as a nurse to support the members of the faith community.

Supporting Sources

Church Health Center: http://www.churchhealthcenter.org/

United Methodist Church Spiritual Gifting Assessment: http://www.umc.org/what-we-believe/spiritual-gifts-online-assessment

Congregational Survey: http://www.healthierchurch.org/wp-content/uploads/2012/07/CHS-Hard-Copy.pdf

REFERENCES
https://www.biblegateway.com/

Made in the USA
Middletown, DE
13 May 2017